Nuggets of Gold

from
The Supreme Being

for
The Starved Soul

Volume 1

SupremeRealityGuide
Birinder Bhullar

D1393089

Introduction

Nuggets of Gold from the Supreme Being
is a revealed piece of guidance to guide
the journey of the Self through life, to
experience Reality.

People in the world of today have drifted
far away into the Un-Real. The appeal of
the sensory and illusory has pulled and held
them. "Gold of Reality" has gone extinct in
the Self, life, and the world. It has lost value
altogether.

Knowing the Spiritual Reality is necessary
for purposeful existence. The human mind,
when it is reasoning against Reality, becomes
blind. It goes into confusion, conflict, dis-
order, and it degenerates. Suffering follows.
This is prevailing in the world now. Deluded
people inebriated with illusion are unwilling
to accept they are going wrong and change.

The new order and way of living in the world
is denial of Reality. Being ignorant about
Reality is one thing; disregarding it and gloat-
ing is another. People have forgotten what

kind of end came in the past, every time the world disrespected Reality.

At present, the Self, Earth, and Nature have all been affected by human disrespect for Reality. Earth is a wonderful place. It has unlimited resources, enough for the needs of everyone here. But human greed is exploiting, plundering, poisoning, and destroying Earth and Nature.

Our world is in a primitive stage of evolution. It is still driven by fear, not by Reality. There is conflict, inner and outer, and need for power.

People get their fake happiness by experiencing might, through subduing others, opposing life, and becoming unnatural. First people break laws of life and create problems. Then they feel mighty trying to solve self-created problems in unnatural ways. People do not realize everything has a limit. Everything comes to a crisis. One day you end up creating a monster you cannot tame.

We are living in a time when the hold of the deluded mind is strong and growing, and the veil of ignorance is very thick. People are drawing their purpose of life, and fake happiness, from deluded existence. It is a critical time for finding Reality.

Turnaround Toward Reality:

Eventually, only after experiencing suffering and futility, a Self becomes willing to turn around toward Spiritual Reality.

But be careful you do not leave a material illusion and enter a spiritual one. Spirituality today is in the marketplace. Many fake spiritual teachers and fake solutions are being offered. Not every teacher or process is real. Human greed has not spared even Truth.

People disillusioned with material living are blindly seeking spirituality for relief. You could become mystified and carried away by a wrong kind. Currently there is a fascination in the West for the East. One misconception is that a visit to the Himalayas, or anything seeming to be from there, will help you encounter the spiritual. This illusion is being packaged and marketed very effectively in the West, and has found a big market.

Undoubtedly the Eastern cultures, especially the Himalayas, have a lot to offer spiritually. But not every yogi or lama there or coming from there is real—and competent to guide a spiritual process. Good reason and results should decide, not beliefs.

Genuine spiritual guidance clarifies, inspires, and frees you first to enter real living. So make sure the process you are being given is not taking you away from real life and that it has transformed and enriched the lives of those who have practiced it before you.

Every Self inherently has both a desire for Spiritual Reality and a resistance to leave the material. To clarify this area for ending fear, I want to reveal: Spiritual Reality is not somewhere else. It only requires transforming your existing Reality, by living a life having awareness, love, and trust. The gold you seek is already there in your existing Self and life. It is mixed with sand of illusions and delusions.

You have to sift it out by hard work. You do not have to leave or go anywhere.

You have lived a long time without knowing Spiritual Reality, and have created fake structures. Such living has disordered and weakened your Self. It is causing pain and suffering in your life. However, you are attached to the unreal and unwilling to accept and let it go. You need clarity, inspiration, and trust to become free. You need a purpose in life you love. You need a way that gives you happiness.

You react, not respond, to every present moment. Past conditioning causes this. You have pre-decided what will give you pleasure or pain: what you will accept or avoid. You have judged and labeled everything. By doing so you have destroyed your openness to experience Reality. But nothing is the same, ever. A thing that gives you pleasure one day could give you pain another day. You live in thought, not in Reality. This is the mind. To enter real living, work to free your Self from the mind and its past beliefs.

You cannot seek what you do not know exists. *Nuggets of Gold* will reveal the Spiritual Reality to you and help you to trust it. It will make you see your existing bondage, inspire you to find a quality of consciousness within your mind that is real—and become happy, and free. From there you may travel any distance toward the Supreme Reality you desire. *Nuggets of Gold* will bring a light in the dark space of your mind. Just a small flame can vanquish darkness. Darkness is no match for pure consciousness.

I Guide a Way Through Living:

You are here to live. Your core desire is to experience Reality. How can you leave living? How can you choke living by misunderstood spirituality of the Self?

Love living. Living is the only process. Find the Gold of Reality in your Self and life. You are unique. You have to find your own gold. It will give you the experience you seek. You can find Happiness, Freedom, and Peace while living where you are.

You have an inseparable relationship with living. You are here for living to experience your Reality. You and life are companions and a team in this process. Sometimes life will pose a question and you will answer; at other times you will pose a question and life will answer. Love life, and you will enter this beautiful relationship and dynamic of true living and learning. So to find the Gold of Reality, this right relationship between you and life has to be found. You have to trust life, not defend against or fear it. You must develop the trust to accept and the ability to read the questions that life poses and the answers it reveals.

The more you live by loving life, the easier the way becomes toward your freedom. The more you complain about something in your life, the more you suffer. Life knows best what to give to you. Let life guide you.

The need for one-on-one guidance with a living guide may arise at a later stage. First live the Reality of life and find spiritual maturity. At some stage a deeper quest for experiencing Supreme Reality will arise. That is not where anyone should begin.

This Book:

The purpose of this book, Volume One in the series, and those that will follow is to reveal and guide you toward a True Reality you do not know. It will give you small morsels of Reality. These truths about Reality I have called *Nuggets of Gold*. The gold was revealed by the Supreme Being. The gold has further gone through the alchemical processes of life, in my life, my family's, who are devoted seekers, and some students I have been guiding for over seven years in the United States. Living has simplified the guidance to a simple, everyday level.

This book will help you find the courage and trust to live from your heart and find your unique Self. It will guide you to integrate seeking Reality with your current life.

1

We want the gold

In everything we seek.

The gold in life is:

Reality.

Gold of Reality has been lost

In the sand of Un-Reality.

We will have to learn

To recognize the gold

And sift it

Out of sand.

2

The gold

In life

Is

The Reality.

And

The way

To find it is:

True and Real Living.

3

The Gold of Reality

Like the metal gold

Makes us spiritually rich

And gives us happiness

And we want unlimited

Quantities of it.

But the Gold of Reality

Also gives us:

Contentment, Freedom, and Clarity—

The metal does not.

4

The Supreme Truth is:

Life is a journey

Through Creation:

You are in it

To experience Reality:

From the Self

To

The Supreme Being.

You are

The traveler.

5

Any journey

We begin from home

And come back home

After fulfilling our purpose.

The Supreme Reality

Is

Our Home.

6

Gold of Reality

Can only be recognized

And sifted from

The infinite Sands of Reality

By a trusting and hardworking Self.

You will have to

Know about your Self

And live in a pure way

To find the Supreme Gold.

7

You do not know

Your Self.

You have lost it

In an ocean of thought

Within your mind.

8

Your present Self is:

Thoughts of your mind.

You have become:

A mind Self

9

Journey of life

Is for experiencing

You will have to enter

Actual living

And not exist

In a thought Reality.

10

Knowing

Your Heart

Is essential.

Without loving something

How will

You live?

So find your heart

And

Know your heart.

11

A mind Self

Is thought:

Memory of the past

And projections

Into the future.

12

There is no freedom

If you live in thought.

Only actual experience

Will give you freedom.

13

You think your Reality:

You live in thought.

You do not know

What love is.

Love is not

What you think.

14

How will you

Love

Without knowing

What love is?

What you think

Is love

Is not love.

15

Your mind is

Your Master:

It rules your heart.

You are no longer living

From your heart.

16

Mind is thought:

Thought is wavering.

Mind can have

No lasting purpose.

Mind can never

Be in joy

Till mind becomes free

From Itself:

By knowing

Its Reality.

17

Your life has become

Only problems:

Problems you created

In the past.

How will you solve them

When

You are still using

The same old

Unclear thinking

And poor reasoning

That caused them?

18

You have reason:

But it is not true.

If you had true reason

You would be free.

Purify

Your reason first

By knowing about Reality.

19

Your reason

Can never be good

Till you have

The gold of

Good intent

In your heart.

20

Till you see

And accept

That you are loving

Un-truthfulness

And illusions

You cannot find

Good intent

And

Good reason.

21

Live

From your heart.

But living from the heart

Is dangerous

If you do not

Have good intentions

And if you do not

Have good reason.

22

To become

A good human being:

Find good reason.

Good reason

Will protect

Your goodness

And protect

Your Self

Against losing

Your way when tempted.

23

Grow virtues

Of your Self.

Do not

Get your

Pleasure from

Wrongdoings:

They will destroy

Your Self.

24

To find your heart

Feel your heart.

First step is:

To become free

From your mind's desires

With true reason.

25

Without:

Love, Faith, and Reason

You will

Not find

Your unique Self:

Your unique Self

Is in your heart.

It is your real love.

26

Any revelation

Or

Any knowledge:

If it does not

Clarify you—

And grow your freedom

To live

It is of no use.

Question it.

27

Your uniqueness

Is your real Self.

It is hidden

In your heart.

Find it

To live

A happy life.

Only it will make

You

Content.

28

Your

Real happiness

Will come

From doing

What you love:

Not the result you get.

29

Once you know

Your heart's love

Resist greed for things

That are not

Your heart's choice.

Why should they

Affect you

Once you know

Your heart's love?

30

Your purpose

Will come

From your love.

Being in love

Is

The most

Powerful way

Toward

What you want.

31

If you desire

To experience

What you love—

But it is

Not happening:

You are

Not loving

What you love

Enough.

32

When in danger

You say, "Supreme Being, save me."

If in the end

You have to

Come to The Supreme Being:

Why deny first?

Either love and relate always

Or never do.

If you are not true

Even with the Supreme Being—

With whom will you be?

33

What was caused

By something

Will also be healed

By the same thing.

This is a Law of Creation.

Your pains and wounds

Of thousands of lives

Life will heal

When you trust

And love life.

34

Only Fire liberates
The gold in you.

Only Fire is the element
That transforms.

To cook food
You need fire.

To melt and shape a metal
You need fire.

To purify your Self
You need fire.

Love and reason are
The purifying fire.

35

Just be in love:

The fire of love

And its reason will

Purify you

And

Consume your fear and doubt.

36

To love something

Go near it.

To go near something

Love it.

37

In love

You desire:

To experience

More and more—

Of what you love.

When you experience

What you love—

You are in joy.

38

Only in Love:

Intent is Pure.

Also pure is attention.

And effortless.

Attentiveness gives joy.

And experience

Becomes real.

39

To know

Your Self:

Constantly grow

And excel

Your Self.

And you will—

Experience your Self.

40

Pride in

Your Self

Is loving

A Self-Image

Not

Your real Self.

41

A better lover

A better loved

A better friend

A better husband

A better wife

A better parent

A better child

A better driver on the road

Be better

In everything you do.

And love your Self and others.

42

Life is a flow:

Water in a pond

And water in a river

Are both water

But are very different.

One is in flow;

The other is stagnant.

Do not let your life

Become stagnant

In any moment

Like a pond.

43

Learn to love

From a child:

A child loves

Only one toy—

Never two

At one time.

44

Only in love

You desire:

To surrender and sacrifice—

And become selfless.

Only in love

Your constant pain is:

You are not loving enough—

Experiencing your love enough—

And not giving enough.

45

Always watch

Your mind for pride:

The human mind

Loves pride.

Only pride gives the mind happiness.

Mind loves pride so much

It does not even want

Grace from The Supreme Being.

A proud mind chooses

To struggle

To feel happiness.

46

Your pride blocks

Grace from The Supreme Being.

Life occasionally

Humbles you

To free you from your pride

To make you experience

Your power is too little—

And grace is

The only answer.

47

Life has laws

Which will always be

More powerful than all your might.

You cannot oppose and win

Against laws of life.

Accept them and live

Without resisting

And struggling.

48

Giving is always

Rewarded by life.

The more you give

The more you are given.

49

Laws of life

Are its justice.

You cannot

Fool life and escape.

Life wants

You to become

A good human being:

And find your Reality.

50

Be good always.

You will become inside

What you do outside.

Otherwise someday

When you will

Want to change:

Purification

Will not be easy.

51

Never be dishonest

With those you love.

Never hide the truth from them

Thinking truth will hurt—

And fearing they

Might leave you.

If you do, you will

Deprive those you love

And your Self

Of Reality.

52

You need a purpose

From your heart

Not from the world:

A purpose

Given to you by the world

Will never give you joy.

You will lose interest in it

And it will not sustain.

53

Only those things that

Enrich your Self

Can make you happy.

Only those things

Make you happy.

Those are done with love.

Things you do

From a compulsion

Never grow your Self.

54

Never try

To be

More compassionate than:

The Supreme Being.

You will

Become fake.

55

When you do something

From your heart

Thought takes over

And says,

"Don't be a fool, this is risky.

Think again, and correct it."

And a good beginning is destroyed.

That is why faith is required

To live from the heart.

56

Goodness is something else—

Trying to be seen as good

Is something else.

There is a big difference.

When you are

Acting to be seen as good

And someone says

The smallest thing

That opposes you:

How quickly

You lose your goodness.

57

Real and lasting change

Comes through small steps

And sincere and sustained work:

Not bridging too far or

Cutting corners.

When you want

To shed old habits:

Take small steps

And have patience.

58

Reason is double-edged:

Be careful

How you use it.

You can create bondage with it

Or set your Self free.

Reason is good when reason

Defends Truth

And does not let you go wrong.

Reason is bad when reason

Opposes Truth

And defends your untruthfulness.

59

Many wealthy people

Before they die

Give all their wealth

For helping others.

Would it not be better if

You detached a little

When younger

And shared your wealth from love

Instead of compulsion

Or guilt at the end

And personally experience

Loving and helping others?

60

The moment you begin

Seeking Reality and becoming your Self—

Everyone begins opposing you

As if you are

Committing a crime.

But when you are

Doing a wrong thing

Very few stop you.

People around you want

You to be dependent on them

And use you

And continue calling it love.

61

Most people think

Becoming spiritual means

Leaving the material.

That is not true.

The material is also spiritual.

Spirituality of the Self

Is not something that

You can separate from material life.

How can you love the spirit

And hate matter

When they are one being?

62

Life is not random.

When you are given a life

Everything is appropriately selected.

You may need

To be born rich or poor,

Healthy or handicapped,

To learn a certain lesson.

Accordingly, parents, children,

Friends, other relationships,

Religion, and culture are given.

63

Happiness is not

The result of something

You do in a certain way.

Happiness exists before

You enter an act.

Happiness is

The Universal Content.

If you want to be happy:

You have to learn to live

In a true way.

64

Most of your energy

Is engaged in

Complaining and questioning.

Why something is

In your life or

Why something is what it is?

The world is unhappy because

People do this all the time.

Where is the time

To love, and live?

65

Fear and faith

Cannot be there

At the same time.

Faith accepts life unconditionally.

Fear does not want you to accept

What you do not want to happen.

Our world is driven by fear:

It is in a very primitive

Stage of existence.

That is why there is

So much need for power in the world.

66

You first analyze,

Make a conclusion

Then you feel safe

To step into life.

In such living

There is no real experience

And no freedom and happiness.

That is why you repeatedly change

From one thing to another.

67

Know it:

Whatever happens in our life

Is in the power of

The Supreme Power,

Which created life and you.

So why fear?

If the Supreme Power

Wants to end us

We can have no defense.

68

Look at a little child playing:

There is no fear

And no tension.

Gradually, parents and society

Instill fear in the child

In the name of wisdom

And teach

Not to accept and trust life.

And true relationship

With life is lost.

And the joy in life is lost.

69

Love, Faith, Reason

Happiness, Freedom, and Peace

Your mind cannot manufacture

With its thoughts.

All these are transcendent.

70

Do not keep your feet

In two boats:

Nothing will work in life

And you will be

Neither here nor there.

Feel your heart

And know which boat

You love more—

And step into it.

Otherwise, there will be

No living and no happiness.

71

Science and philosophy

Have freed us from

Ignorance and savagery,

Rituals and witchcraft

Of the dark ages.

But they are not complete

For finding the Reality of life:

Only Love and Faith

Have the infinite reach.

72

We cannot

Experience anything

Unless we are

In a sincere quest.

And we cannot

Experience anything

Deeper than our real questions.

73

Meditation is to

Gather you to feel your Self.

It alone cannot

Take you across

To the Supreme Reality.

If you want to seek Supreme Reality

You have to live and purify as well.

74

Asking mind questions

Those that have not arisen

From living

Grows only knowledge

And thought.

Reality of your Self

You cannot grasp by thought.

75

What surety do you have

The Sun will rise tomorrow?

You never think this:

Take it as a given

And unconsciously continue to trust

And live.

But when accepting Supreme Reality

Is suggested

You find it irrational to trust

And you vehemently oppose.

76

Next time something happens—

Even the most ordinary—

See it deeply

And ask your Self:

How much of what happened

Did I cause

And how much

Did I not?

It will humble you

If you can see.

77

To seek anything:

Past knowledge guides.

To recognize anything:

Past knowledge guides.

But nothing will ever happen

Like anything in the past.

So Faith is essential

To accept

The Unknown

And to live to evolve.

78

Countless miracles

Keep you living.

Look at just one of them:

Your heart is beating day and night

To keep you living.

What is your doing in it?

You only become conscious

When it skips a beat.

As long as life goes well

You think it is your doing

And you live unconscious

Of the miracles and grace.

79

Your mind feels secure

Only in the known.

Your mind feels confident

Only in repetition.

That is why

Your mind wants the past to repeat.

But life never

Repeats an expression.

Life is ever new.

Fear cannot end till

You have Faith.

80

Earth is

Such a wonderful place.

There are so many resources.

Enough for everyone living

To be well provided for and happy forever.

All you have to do is

Step out of the way of Nature

And stop exploiting, plundering, and
poisoning

Nature with your science.

Nature will heal itself

The damage you have done

Your ignorant wisdom will destroy further.

81

Silence does not mean

You are not talking.

Silence means you have

A silent mind:

You have a mind free from thought.

You could be silent while talking

Or you could be

Talking while silent.

Only love can make you silent.

Love makes you silent the fastest.

82

I have always taught:

Even ninety-nine percent

Love and Faith

Is not yet real Love and Faith.

If water is at one hundred feet:

By ninety-nine feet of digging

You will not find water.

83

Your Courage

Is a measure of

How much you love.

Heart-centered people

Are courageous.

Mind-centered people

Are never free of fear.

84

Your pride

Has destroyed you.

Pride is the deadliest monster.

If you love a monster,

Live with a monster,

Sleep with a monster,

It is going to

Eat you up

Sooner or later.

Kill it as quickly as possible.

And become free.

85

What is the guarantee:

Your heart will beat one more time,

Your next breath will come?

What is the guarantee:

The person who

Loves you today

Will love you tomorrow?

Only relating

With life from faith

Will make you feel secure

In unpredictability.

86

Feeling insecure in life

Is natural.

Accept it.

Do not hide it.

If there is no insecurity

How will faith come?

87

When you ask

For ten steps

Toward something

You are not

On the path

Of Love and Faith.

It is a need of the mind

To know everything.

88

Your Self

Has lost trust in you.

Your Self has become

Unresponsive to you.

You have starved it

Too long for Reality.

Till you can

Find a love

And live for it

Your Self will not revive.

89

Happiness of the mind is

Creating a problem

And then solving the problem to feel great.

Pull out a slice of twenty years

From any time

And divide it

Into two equal periods:

You will see

What the world did in the first ten years,

It reversed in the next ten.

This is mind living.

90

Crying is very freeing.

It is sincerely accepting

You are in pain

And want

Your Reality to change.

Hiding pain hardens you.

91

When you

Do not want to

Give your own Self

Its freedom

Why should anyone

Give you freedom?

The first step toward

Your Self-freedom is:

Give your Self Freedom.

92

Not choosing

Is the cause of

Your unhappiness.

Unhappiness

Begins lessening

The very moment

You make a choice.

Try it.

93

Life puts

Gold of Reality

Before you

Every moment.

You have your own ideas

And want your control.

You do not trust

And recognize love of life

And miss it.

94

Running away

From suffering

Is choosing not to live.

Running away

From suffering

Is saying no

To the gold of Reality

Life has for you.

95

Without Love

And courage

You cannot

Enter real living.

Add Faith and clarity

And you have

Everything needed

For living well.

96

Ask yourself

At the beginning

Of every day:

"How am I going to live today

Better than yesterday?"

And ask yourself

At the end

Of every day:

"Did I live today

Better than yesterday?"

97

To become truly wealthy

Grow your spiritual wealth as well.

Material wealth

Is transient.

And will end

With life here.

98

Give your Self

The freedom

To make mistakes.

Your Self-image

Is frightened

To make mistakes.

This is

Your bondage:

Which is not

Letting you live.

99

Be Truthful

With your Self

And the world:

And

Live

Sincerely.

Life will not trust you

Otherwise.

100

Creation and life

Owe you nothing.

You owe everything

You have to them.

Let this humble you—

If you want to truly live.

101

Patience is essential.

Spring comes after one year.

Regardless how hard you work

And how much care you take

Of a plant—

For bloom you have to wait

For spring to come.

Natural cycles follow laws:

And their own course.

102

Unlimited knowledge is

Freely available in the world today.

The mind has become addicted to it.

Such indiscriminately gathered

Secondhand knowledge

Has made minds of today

Vain, indecisive, and confused.

Self-knowledge has to be Self-grown:

Through living and experiencing—

And leads to Self-Knowing.

103

Say the word

Sweet or bitter:

It will give you a real feeling.

But the word Self will not:

Say the word Self and feel.

People ask, "What is the Self?"

People never ask, "What is sweet or bitter?"

This shows you need to live

And experience

Your Self.

Afterword

If I had to share just three words of guidance—and repeat a thousand times, to emphasize their absolute beauty, power, and significance—that can bring any Self to unique blossoming in life, those would be:

Love

Faith

Reason

This is Supreme Gold amongst the Nuggets of Gold.

SupremeRealityGuide

Birinder Bhullar

CPSIA information can be obtained
at www.ICGtesting.com
Printed in the USA
FFHW020758050119
50064179-54881FF